David McLeod-Jones

Investigating a Group of New Zealand Leaders

David McLeod-Jones

Investigating a Group of New Zealand Leaders

Roots of, Routes to, and Routines in Leadership.

VDM Verlag Dr. Müller

Imprint

Bibliographic information by the German National Library: The German National Library lists this publication at the German National Bibliography; detailed bibliographic information is available on the Internet at http://dnb.d-nb.de.

Any brand names and product names mentioned in this book are subject to trademark, brand or patent protection and are trademarks or registered trademarks of their respective holders. The use of brand names, product names, common names, trade names, product descriptions etc. even without a particular marking in this works is in no way to be construed to mean that such names may be regarded as unrestricted in respect of trademark and brand protection legislation and could thus be used by anyone.

Cover image: www.purestockx.com

Publisher:
VDM Verlag Dr. Müller Aktiengesellschaft & Co. KG , Dudweiler Landstr. 125 a, 66123 Saarbrücken, Germany,
Phone +49 681 9100-698, Fax +49 681 9100-988,
Email: info@vdm-verlag.de

Zugl.: Auckland, Massey University, 2004

Produced in USA and UK by:
Lightning Source Inc., La Vergne, Tennessee, USA
Lightning Source UK Ltd., Milton Keynes, UK
BookSurge LLC, 5341 Dorchester Road, Suite 16, North Charleston, SC 29418, USA

ISBN: 978-3-639-01681-9

Investigating a group of New Zealand leaders: their roots of, routes to, and routines in leadership.

To Susan, Samuel and Elizabeth – the company I keep at home will always be more important to me than any company I lead. Thanks for your love and support.

CONTENTS

ACKNOWLEDGEMENTS

I would like to acknowledge the time the participants in my research project gave so freely from their busy lives to be interviewed.

I would like to acknowledge my employer for their generosity in funding and time that they have provided to allow me to complete this project.

INTRODUCTION

Zaleznik (1977) addressing "Development of leadership" in *Managers and leaders: Are they different?* states that, "The development of every person begins in the family . . . Also, beyond early childhood, the patterns of development that affect managers and leaders involve the selective influence of particular people (p.75). This leads to a position of leadership that he earlier suggested, "inevitably requires using power to influence the thoughts and actions of people" (p.67).

These stages of leadership correspond with the roots of leadership, the routes to leadership, and the routines in leadership, investigated in this research project. These were drawn, with some modification, from research conducted by Sinclair and Wilson (2002) into leadership in the Australian setting.

Having observed the impact of leadership, or the lack of, in both work and community settings, I was interested to investigate what led to a person becoming a leader, and what they thought they did in that role.

It was only near the end of my literature review that I came across Sinclair and Wilson's work and their use of qualitative research for investigating leadership. I have modelled my research project on theirs, to investigate the development and practises of a group of leaders in the New Zealand setting.

LITERATURE REVIEW

APPROACHES TO RESEARCHING LEADERSHIP

Stogdill (1974) in a review of leadership research points out that there are almost as many different approaches to "leadership" as there are people who have tried to define it (p.7). Northouse (2004) has summarised the most common approaches to researching leadership, measures developed, and the positive and negative features of each approach.

The trait approach

This approach to researching leadership was the first systematic attempt to study characteristics of leaders. In the early part of the 20th century traits were studied to determine what made certain people great leaders. The theories that were developed were called "great man" theories because they focussed on identifying the innate qualities and characteristics possessed by certain great social, political and military leaders e.g. Gandhi, Lincoln and Napoleon. It was believed that people were born with these traits and only the "great" people possessed them.

Although the research on traits spanned the entire 20th century, a good overview of this research is found in two surveys of trait studies completed by Stogdill (1948, 1974). His results showed that the average leader is different from the average group member in the following ways: (a) intelligence (b) alertness (c) insight (d) responsibility (e) initiative (f) persistence (g) self-confidence (h) sociability.

Mann (1959) conducted a similar study that examined more than 1,400 findings regarding personality and leadership in small groups. Mann suggested that personality traits could be used to discriminate leaders from non-leaders. His results identified leaders as strong in the following traits: intelligence, masculinity, adjustments, dominance, extroversion and conservatism. Lord et al. (1986) reassessed the findings of Mann using the process of meta-analysis, and found that intelligence, masculinity and dominance were significantly related to how individuals perceived leaders.

Kirkpatrick and Locke (1991) contended that "it is unequivocally clear that leaders are not like other people" (p.59). From a qualitative synthesis of earlier research, Kirkpatrick and Locke postulated that leaders differ from non-leaders on six traits: drive, the desire to lead, honesty and integrity, self-confidence, cognitive ability, and the knowledge of the business.

One of the most common measures has been the Leadership Trait Questionnaire (LTQ). The LTQ quantifies the perception of the individual leader and selected observers, such as subordinates and peers. It measures an individual's traits and points the individual to those areas in which they may have special strengths or weaknesses.

There are several positive aspects of the trait approach to leadership. First, it is intuitively appealing because it fits clearly the popular idea that leaders are people who are out front, leading the way in society Secondly, there is a century of research that validates the basis of this perspective. Third, by focussing exclusively on the leader, the trait approach provides an in-depth approach to the leader component in the leadership process. Last, it has provided some benchmarks against which individuals can evaluate their personal leadership attributes.

On the negative side, the trait approach had failed to delimit a definitive list of leadership traits. In analysing the traits of leaders, the approach has failed to take into account the impact of situations. In addition, the approach has resulted in subjective lists of the important leadership traits, which are not necessarily grounded in strong, reliable research. Furthermore, the trait approach has not adequately linked the traits of leaders with other outcomes such as group and team performance. Last, this approach is not particularly useful for training and development of leadership because individual's personal attributes are relatively stable and fixed, and therefore their traits are not amenable to change.

The skills approach

This approach to researching leadership began with an article published by Robert Katz in the *Harvard Business Review* in 1955, titled "Skills for an Effective Administrator." Katz's article appeared at a time when researchers were trying to identify a definitive set of leadership traits. Katz's approach was an attempt to transcend the trait problem by addressing leadership as a set of developed skills. More recently, a renewed interest in a skills commonality has emerged. Beginning in the 1990s, a multitude of studies have been published that contend that a leader's effectiveness depends on the leader's ability to solve complex organisational problems. This research has resulted in a comprehensive skill-based model of leadership that was advanced by Mumford and his colleagues (Mumford, Zaccaro, Harding, Jacobs & Fleishman, 2000; Yammarino, 2000).

Based on his observations of executives in the workplace, Katz suggested that effective leaders commonly use three basic personal skills: technical, human, and conceptual (p.34). Katz argued that these skills are quite different from traits or qualities of leaders. Skills imply what leaders can accomplish, whereas traits imply who leaders are. Technical skill is having knowledge about and being proficient in a type of work or activity. It requires competencies in a specialised area, analytical ability, and the ability to use appropriate tools and techniques. Human skill is having knowledge about and being able to work with people. Human skills are 'people skills.' They are the abilities that help a leader work effectively with subordinates, peers, and superiors to successfully accomplish the organisation's goals. Conceptual skills are abilities to work with ideas and concepts. A leader with conceptual skills is comfortable talking about the ideas that shape an organisation and the intricacies involved.

There are many questionnaires that assess an individual's skills for leadership. Most all of them are designed to be used in training and development to give people a feel for their leadership ability. Most are not used in research because they have not been tested for reliability and validity. Most recent of those that do fit this criteria is that developed by Mumford and his colleagues (2000) which includes open-ended responses and sophisticated scoring procedures.

There are several positive features to conceptualising leadership from a skills approach. First, it is a leader-centred model that stresses the importance of the leader's abilities, and it places learned skills at the centre of effective leadership performance. Second, the skills approach describes leadership in such a way that it makes it available to everyone. Skills are competencies that we can all learn to develop and improve upon. Third, the skills approach provides a sophisticated map that explains how effective leadership performance can be achieved. Last, this approach provides a structure for leadership education and development programs that include creative problem solving, conflict resolution, listening and teamwork.

In addition to the positive features, there are also some negative aspects to the skills approach. First, the breadth of the model seems to extend beyond the boundaries of leadership, including, for example, conflict management, critical thinking, motivational theory, and personality theory. Second, the skills model is weak in predictive value. It does not explain how a person's competencies lead to effective leadership performance. Third, the skills model claims not to be a trait approach, but individual traits such as cognitive abilities, motivation, and personality play a large role in the model. Finally, the skills model is weak in its general application because it was constructed using only data from military personnel.

The style approach

This approach to researching leadership determined that leaders exhibit two kinds of behaviours: task behaviours and relationship behaviours. Task behaviours facilitate goal accomplishment: they help group members to achieve objectives. Relationship behaviours help subordinates feel comfortable with themselves, with each other, and with the situation they find themselves in.

Many studies have been conducted to investigate a style orientation. Some of the first studies to be done were conducted at Ohio State University (Hemphill & Coons, 1957), based on the findings of Stogdill's (1948) work, which pointed to the importance of considering more than leaders' traits. At the same time, another group of researchers at the University of Michigan (Cartwright & Zander, 1960) was conducting a series of studies that explored how leaders functioned in small groups. A third line of research was begun by Blake and Mouton (1964), it explored how mangers used task and relationship behaviours in an organisational setting.

The two most commonly used measures have been the Leader Behaviour Description Questionnaire-LBDQ (Stogdill, 1963) and the Leadership Grid (Blake and McCanse, 1991). Both of these measures provide information about the degree to which leaders act task directed and people directed. The LBDQ was designed primarily for research and had has been used extensively since the 1960s. the Leadership Grid was designed primarily for training and development, and it continues to be used today for training managers and supervisors in the leadership process.

The style approach has several positive features. First, it has broadened the scope of leadership research to include the study of the behaviour of leaders rather than only their personal traits or characteristics. Second, it is a reliable approach because it is supported by a wide range of studies. Third, the style approach is valuable because it underscores the importance of the two core dimensions of leadership behaviour: task and relationship. Fourth, it has heuristic value in that it provides us with a broad conceptual map that is useful in gaining an approach of our own leadership behaviours.

On the negative side, researchers have not been able to associate the behaviours of leaders (task and relationship) with outcomes such as morale, job satisfaction, and productivity. In addition, researchers from the style approach have not been able to identify a universal set of leadership behaviours that would consistently result in effective leadership. Last, the style approach implies, but fails to support fully, the idea that the most effective leadership style is a high-high style (i.e. high task and high relationship.

The situational approach

This approach to researching leadership investigated the way leaders behave in different situations. It stresses that leaders behave both in a directive and supportive dimension. To determine what is needed in a particular situation, a leader must evaluate their employees and assess how competent and committed they are to perform a given task. Then the leader must match their style to the competence and commitment of the subordinates. Effective leaders have in common the ability to recognise what employees need and then adapt their own style to meet those needs.

Research was conducted by Hersey and Blanchard (1969) based on Reddin's (1967) 3D management style theory. This research has been refined and revised several times since its inception (Hersey & Blanchard, 1977; Blanchard, Zigarmi, & Zigrami, 1985) and it has been used extensively in organisational leadership training and development.

Although different versions of instruments have been used to measure situational leadership, nearly all of them are constructed similarly. As a rule, the questionnaire provides a series of 12 to 20 work-related situations and asks respondents to select their preferred style for each situation from four alternatives. The situations and styles are written so as to directly represent the leadership styles of the four quadrants in the model. Questionnaire responses are scored so as to give individuals information about their primary and secondary leadership styles, their flexibility, and their leadership effectiveness.

There are four positive features to the situational approach. Foremost, it is an approach to measuring leadership that is widely recognised as a standard for training leaders. Second, it is a practical approach that is easily understood and easily applied. Third, this approach sets forth a clear set of prescriptions for how leaders should act if they want to enhance their leadership effectiveness. Fourth, situational leadership recognises and stresses that there is not one best style of leadership, instead, leaders need to be flexible and adapt their style to the requirements of the situation.

The situational leadership approach has negative features that may prove to be limitations. Unlike many other leadership approaches, this approach does not have a strong body of research findings to justify and support the theoretical underpinnings on which it stands. As a result, there is ambiguity regarding how the approach conceptualises certain aspects of the leadership process. It is not clear in explaining how subordinates move from low development levels to high development levels, nor is it clear about how commitment changes over time for subordinates. Without the basic research findings, the validity of the basic prescriptions for matching leader styles to subordinates development levels must also be questioned. Finally, in applying this approach, there are not guidelines for how leaders use this approach in group settings as opposed to one-to-one contexts.

The contingency approach

This approach to researching leadership arose from the work of Fiedler (1964). The contingency approach is a leadership match theory (Fiedler & Chemers, 1974) which means it tries to match leaders to appropriate situations. It is called contingency because it suggests that a leader's effectiveness depends on how well the leader's style fits the context. To understand the performance of leaders, it is essential to understand the situations in which they lead. Effective leadership is contingent on matching a leader's style to the right setting.

Fiedler developed contingency theory by studying the styles of many different leaders who worked in different contexts, primarily military organisations. He assessed leader's styles, the situations in which they worked, and whether or not they were effective. After analysing the styles of hundreds of leaders who were both good and bad, Fiedler and his colleagues were able to make empirically grounded generalisations about which styles of leadership were best and which styles were worst for a given organisational context.

Fiedler developed the Least Preferred Co-Worker (LPC) measure. The LPC scale is used to measure a person's leadership style. For example, it measures your style by having you describe a co-worker with whom you have had difficulty completing a task. This does not need to be a co-worker you disliked a great deal, but rather someone with whom you least like to work. After you have selected this individual, the LPC scale asks you to describe your co-worker on 18 sets of adjectives.

The positive features of the contingency approach include that it is backed by a considerable amount of research, it is the first measure to emphasise the impact of situation on leaders, it is predictive of leadership effectiveness, it allows leaders not to be effective in all situations, and it can provide useful leadership profile data.

On the negative side, the contingency approach can be criticised because it has not adequately explained the link between styles and situations, and it relies heavily on the LPC scale, which has been questioned for its face validity and workability. Finally it does not fully explain how organisations can use the results in situational engineering.

The path-goal approach

This approach to researching leadership draws heavily from studies into what motivates employees and first appeared in leadership literature in the early 1970s in the work of Evans (1970), House and Dessler (1974) and House and Mitchell (1974). For the leader, the challenge is to use a leadership style that best meets subordinates' motivational needs. This is commonly done by choosing behaviours that complement or supplement what is missing in the work setting. Leaders commonly try to enhance subordinates' goal attainment by providing information or rewards in the work environment (Indvik, 1986); leaders provide subordinates with the elements they think their subordinates need to reach their goal.

According to House and Mitchell (1974), leaders commonly generate motivation when they increase the numbers of the kinds of payoffs that subordinates receive from their work. Leaders also commonly motivate when they make the path to the goal clear and easy to travel through coaching and direction, when they remove obstacles and roadblocks to attaining the goal, and when they make the work itself more personally satisfying. In what became known as path-goal theory it is suggested that whether or not a particular leader behaviour is motivating to subordinates is dependant on the subordinates' characteristics and the characteristics of the task.

Because the path-goal approach was developed as a complex set of theoretical assumptions to direct researchers in developing leadership theory, it has used many different instruments to measure the leadership process. The Path-Goal Leadership Questionnaire illustrates one of the questionnaires that has been useful in measuring and learning about important aspects of path-goal leadership (Indvik, 1988).

Path-goal approach to leadership has several positive features. First, it provides a useful framework for approach how various leadership behaviours affect the satisfaction of subordinates and their work performance. Second, it attempts to integrate the motivational principles of expectancy theory into an approach of leadership. Thirdly, it provides a model that in certain ways is very practical.

The approach also has several identifiable weaknesses. First, the path-goal approach is so complex and incorporates so many different aspects of leadership that interpreting the meaning can be confusing. Secondly, it has received only partial support from empirical research studies that have conducted to test its validity (Schriesheim & Kerr, 1977). Thirdly it has been criticised for failing to explain adequately the relationship between leadership behaviour and worker motivation. Fourthly, it tends to treat leadership as a one way event – the leader affects the subordinate.

The leader-member exchange (LMX) approach

This approach to researching leadership was developed from work by Dansereau, Graen and Haga (1975), who found that leaders commonly group subordinates into either in-groups or out-groups based on how well they work with the leader and how well the leader works with them. In addition, becoming part of one group or the other is based on how subordinates involve themselves in expanding their role responsibility with the leader (Graen, 1976). Subordinates who are interested in negotiating with the leader what they are willing to do for the group can become a part of the in-group. These negotiations involve exchanges in which subordinates do certain activities that can go beyond their formal job descriptions, and the leader, in turn, does more for the subordinate. If subordinates are not interested in taking on new and different job responsibilities, they become part of the out-group.

Many different questionnaires have been used as measures by LMX researchers. An example is the LMX 7, a seven item-questionnaire that provides a reliable and valid measure of the quality of leader-member exchanges (Graen & Uhl-Bien, 1995). The LMX 7 is designed to measure three dimensions of leader-member relationship: respect, trust, and obligation. It assesses the degree to which leaders and followers have mutual respect for each other's capabilities, feel a deep sense of reciprocal trust, and have a strong sense of obligation to each other. Taken together, these dimensions are the ingredients necessary to create strong partnerships.

There are several positive features to the LMX approach. First, it is a strong descriptive approach that explains how leaders use some subordinates (in-group members) more than others (out-group members) to accomplish organisational goals effectively. Secondly it is unique in that, unlike other approaches it makes leader-member relationships the focal point of the leadership process. Related to this focus, it is noteworthy because it directs our attention to the importance of effective communication in leader-member relationships. Last, it is supported by a multitude of studies that link high-quality leader-member exchanges to positive organisational outcomes.

There are also negative features in the LMX approach. Foremost, it runs counter to our principles of fairness and justice in the workplace by suggesting that some members of the work unit receive special attention and others do not. Second it emphasises the importance of leader-member exchanges, but fails to explain the intricacies of how one goes about creating high-quality exchanges. Finally, there are questions regarding whether the principal measure is sufficiently refined to measure the complexities of leadership.

The transformational approach

This approach to researching leadership has been the focus of much work since the early 1980s. As its name implies, transformational leadership is a process that changes and transforms individuals. It is concerned with values, ethics, standards, and long-term goals. These were investigated by Bennis & Nanus (1985) and Tichy & DeVanna (1986). The methods used by these researchers to collect data were quite similar. They simply identify a number of CEOs or leaders at large corporations and then interviewed them, using a relatively unstructured, open-ended question-and-answer format.

Transformational leadership is part of the "New Leadership" paradigm (Bryman, 1992), which gives more attention to the charismatic and affective elements of leadership. In a content analysis of articles published in the *Leadership Quarterly,* Lowe and Gardner (2001) found that one third of the research was about transformation/charismatic leadership.

The most widely used measure is the Multifactor Leadership Questionnaire-MLQ (Bass, 1985). The MLQ is made up of questions that measure the followers' perception of a leaders' behaviour for each of the seven factors in the transformational and transactional models, and it also has items that measure extra effort, effectiveness and satisfaction.

There are several positive features of the transformational approach, including that it is a current model that has received a lot of attention by researchers, it has a strong intuitive appeal, it emphasises the importance of followers in the leadership process, it goes beyond traditional transactional models and broadens leadership to include the growth of followers, and it places strong emphasis on morals and values.

Balancing off the positive features of transformational leadership are several negative features. These include that the approach lacks conceptual clarity, it is often interpreted to simplistically as an either-or approach, it creates a framework that implies that transformational leadership has a trait-like quality, it is sometimes seen as elitist and undemocratic, it is derived from and supported by data that focus on senior-level leaders, and it has the potential to be used counterproductively in negative ways by leaders.

SOME SUGGESTED WEAKNESSES OF THE ABOVE APPROACHES TO RESEARCHING LEADERSHIP

These approaches have not produced a common understanding/definition of leadership

 The biggest weakness of the approaches is that there are so many of them, and yet they have not produced a common understanding/definition of leadership. In the past 50 years there has been as many as 65 different classification systems developed to define the dimensions of leadership (Fleishman et al., 1991).

As an example there is the scheme proposed by Bass (1990, p. 11-20) which highlights a number of understandings/definitions. He suggests that some understandings/definitions of leadership see it as the *focus of group process.*

From this perspective, the leader is at the centre of group change and activity and embodies the group. Another understanding/definition conceptualises leadership from a *personality perspective*, which suggests that leadership is a combination of special traits or characteristics that individuals possess and that enable them to induce other to accomplish tasks. Other understandings/definitions of leadership have defined it as an *act* or *behaviour* – the things leaders do to bring about change in a group.

In addition, leadership has been understood/defined in terms of the *power relationship* that exists between leaders and follower. From this viewpoint, leaders have power and wield it to change others. Others understand/define leadership as an *instrument of goal achievement* in helping group members achieve their goals and needs. This view includes leadership that transforms followers through vision setting, role modelling, and individualised attention. Finally, some scholars understand/define leadership from a *skills perspective*. This viewpoint stresses the capabilities (knowledge and skills) that make effective leadership possible.

Teo (2002) in her Massey University Master of Management thesis *Leadership & Logology* produced a table (adapted from Huczynski, 1993, pp. 32-34) summarising her research, which shows on-going attempts to produce an understanding/definition of leadership during the 1900s:

Date	Author(s)	Labelled	Theory
1900-	Stogdill	Traits	Characteristics of an individual
1940s	Lewin, Lippit	Behavioural	Autocratic, democratic, laissez-faire
1964	Blake, Mouton	Managerial grid	Leadership style
1967	Fiedler	Contingency	Match leader to situation
1970	Greenleaf	Servant	Leader as servant
1977	Hershey, Blanchard	Situational	Match leader style to follower readiness
1985	Bass	Transformational	Expectations exceeded by intervention
1988	DePree	Leadership art	Cultivate positive workplace culture
1991	Covey	Principle-centred	Commitment to values
1993	Block	Stewardship	Accountability
1997	Tichy, Cohen	Leadership engine	Leaders as teacher

Also they have failed to arrive at a clear distinction between managers and leaders. Teo (2002) notes that most research suggests a distinction based on personality types, with the leaders commonly possessing more 'transcendent' traits such as vision, passion and creativity, while manger's traits commonly focus on 'doing' things such as problem solving. Kotter (1990) suggested that leaders create the vision for an organisation, whereas the key function of the manger is to implement the vision. Yet he also argued that managers must know how to lead as well as manage. The classic quote from Warren Bennis says, "Managers are people who do things right, and leaders are people who do the right thing." (1985, p.221). However this may be simplistic, ignoring Nirenberg's (2001) observation that bad mangers are now called 'managers' and good managers are now called 'leaders.'

These approaches are too business focussed

Sinclair and Wilson (2002) point out that in the last few decades there has been a tendency by business management literature to annex the leadership terrain. Where once the study of leadership was carried out in the classics and politics departments, now one is more likely to find professors of leadership in business and management schools. There has been a resulting tendency to conflate business leadership with other forms of leadership and to behave as if corporate leaders share the same characteristics with other sorts of leaders. This has produced theoretical and other problems in the study of leadership. Shamir (1995), in his study of charismatic leadership, points out that much of the research on charisma in corporate leaders has mistakenly extrapolated from studies of charismatic political and religious leaders. The key problem is that political and religious leaders benefit from being distant from followers and not having their charisma put to the close personal scrutiny that we typically measure when we are assessing corporate leaders. According to Shamir's study, close-up charismatic corporate leadership is a fundamentally different phenomenon from the more distant and managed charisma of political and religious leaders.

These approaches are too quantitative

Another trend has been the study of leadership using quantitative methodologies associated with psychology (Parry 1998). Rather than rely on history or biography, or detailed case studies which has been the political scientists' tools of trade, the field of leadership is now dominated by survey and questionnaire techniques and statistical analyses that trade off depth. As Conger (1998, p.109) argues, "most survey-generated leadership descriptors fail to understand the deeper structures of leadership phenomena. We trade-off the 'how' and 'why' questions about leadership for highly abstracted concepts and descriptions which allow us only to generalise . . . at relatively superficial levels." Conger maintains that leadership, as a multiple-level and highly interpretive phenomenon, is more suited to qualitative research methods, including interviews, observation and participant observation. A number of researchers who maintain the need for both qualitative and quantitative studies of leadership point out that despite thousands of quantitative studies, 'this general orientation has not yet led to an enduring and integrative theory of leadership' (Parry 1998; see also Yukl 1994 and Bennis and Nanus 1985).

ONE ALTERNATIVE APPROACH TO RESEARCHING LEADERSHIP

Sinclair and Wilson (2002) conducted research on leadership in 1999 and 2000 as part of a project organised by the Australian Department of Immigration and Multicultural Affairs. The project methodology was qualitative, utilising discursive, narrative interviews to explore ideas about leadership. They chose to investigate three areas. The first was *the roots of leadership,* which investigated the role played by a leader's family of origin. The second was *the routes to leadership,* which investigated the differing pathways taken by the leaders studied. The third, *capabilities and strategies* investigated the daily activities undertaken by leaders. Their findings were published in *New Faces of Leadership* (Melbourne University Press 2002).

The roots of leadership

They found that half of the men had grown up without strong father identification. Their fathers had either died when they were young, or had been away a lot on business, or were emotionally withdrawn from family life. Some of those interviewed simply did not relate to disconnected or remote fathers. Others, coming late in the birth order, lacked the close attention from their father that a first-born son often experiences.

This meant that mothers often played a larger role in their lives, and/or they found other mentors. Consequently, they experienced less of the traditional 'masculine' gender role modelling – with its hierarchical, competitive emphases – and correspondingly more of the female influence, stressing relationships and personal interactions. One man described his upbringing in a particularly female environment: 'My father had a few strokes and was pretty much wrapped up in his own world. So my mother and aunt and grandmother were important figures in my own life . . .'

In his 1983 book, *Leaders We Deserve,* Alistair Mant describes research showing that sons in families where the father was absent for at least two years in childhood developed aptitude scores which looked more like those of intelligent young women. Those with fathers who were present tended to show the typical male bias towards mathematics. Absence of a strong fatherly influence can create, or leave, a space that sets some men free to become more 'creative', or less constrained to adopt conservative forms of masculinity.

In the political sphere, former US President Bill Clinton and UK Prime Minister Tony Blair are described sometimes as 'third way' leaders. By 'third way' is meant a leadership that escapes standard constraint and is based on imagining transforming solutions rather than the transactional deal-making of other leader styles (Little 1999). One of the interesting things about Clinton and Blair is that both had childhoods characterised, one way or another, by insecure father identification. The leadership style these two men contrasts strongly with that of President George W. Bush, whose middle initial is apparently all that separates him from his father and mentor, former President George bush senior. George W. Bush favours the more traditional tough-minded conservatism that is an extension of his father's style.

Leadership studies have traditionally indicated a preponderance of first-born sons in the ranks of leaders in politics, business and society (see for example Mant's discussion: 1983: 45). Studies of women political leaders confirm that an extraordinary high proportion of women in political office consist of first-borns, commonly from all-girl families. Particularly if they don't have any brothers, these women experience a range of influences, including paternal attention and high aspirations, that produce leadership motivations (Stienburg 1998).

Most of Sinclair and Wilson's interviewees came from larger families. Of the fifteen only one was an only child, while eight came from families with four or more children. Three were from three-child families and three were from two-child families, yielding an average of close to four children per family. By contrast, in the general Australian population, only 5 per cent of families have four or more children.

This suggests something about boundaries. The larger the family, the more human boundaries there are to negotiate, and the more one might learn about relationships – the complexities and the subtleties – and about being flexible. While large families might produce fierce attachments to one's own territory, nevertheless the realities of living with several others test those attachments on a daily basis.

Secondly, the majority of their leaders came later in the birth order rather than being the eldest. Nine of ten male interviewees were further down in birth order – third of four, fourth of six, sixth of seven and so on. This suggests that second and subsequent children might become different sorts of leaders – more naturally democratic perhaps. As Alistair Mant (1983) notes, subsequent children in a family have a vested interest in fairness, in fair play and a fair go for all. This links to qualities such as diversity-mindedness, to an empathy with people who lack power, an ability to negotiate pathways, and a desire to see fair play in organisations.

Several of the interviewees had changed countries or changed schools, in some cases several times, exposing them to foreignness and difference and creating the need for adaptability. Mostly, and with the benefit of hindsight, this was an experienced as an enormously positive expanding of outlook and possibility, instilling confidence about moving and an appetite for cultural differences that became a major plank of identity.

People who have thrust themselves, or been thrust by circumstances, into challenging situations without their normal supports often learn new things about themselves. Howard Gardner (1984; 1993) says that highly disruptive experiences of being an outsider can sharpen the intelligences, particularly creative intelligence. It does this by throwing people back on their own resources and giving them the experience of operating without approval of others, being more self-sufficient in terms of esteem and identity needs.

The routes to leadership

Sinclair and Wilson found that more than half of the leaders they interviewed had arrived in their present position from quite different fields. These varied workplace experiences had extended the range of their social and professional lives. For example, two had commenced their working lives in the Commonwealth Employment Service, There they had witnessed the difficulties of unemployment, especially for minority ethnic groups and women.

Several of the leaders had first started work on the factory floor as young engineers, working alongside people of many different nationalities:

> I spent a lot of time on the factory floors. I did a sandwich course – my degree was
> five years but it involved three sessions of six months in industry, on the factory floor
> – so I've been dealing with cultural diversity from day one, especially in my first ten

years of work. There were multiple nationalities. I'm not sure if I'm any good at it bit I'm comfortable working with different cultures.

For those with apparently more predictable careers – largely remaining with the same firm – varied experiences in and out of work hours provided exposure, and insight, into differences. Many started out in jobs where they mixed closely with people of different nationalities and educational backgrounds. One had driven his blind neighbour to his place of work for a couple of years, giving him a keen sense of, and empathy for, those with disability or disadvantage. One engineer had taken his first job with an overseas company in order to travel and be extended.

Variety in occupational setting has provided these leaders with arrange of vantage points from which to view the world of work and relationships. Early professional experiences, which place people in different departments within an organisation, also help in the process of extending mental boundaries as well a extending specific skill ranges. So the engineer who does a stint in the marketing area or in human resources learns new ways of looking at people and problems. They learn that a marketing mindset, for example, is very different from an engineering mindset. It becomes easier to extrapolate to other diverse mindsets. Interviewees enthused about the enrichment they had gained, both personal and professional, from being obliged to work in other departments, even when the transitions had been difficult.

Others commented on the significance of mentor support in early and middle career. Rather than sustained career support, in many cases the mentor's role was simply a bit of good advice or an introduction at a critical time. It is worth adding that, by the time they offer the support, mentors have often had ample evidence that their protégés have special potential.

Sinclair and Wilson suggest that connections can be made between working experience of leadership and earlier workplace experiences. The connections between formative experiences and leadership are especially pertinent in a corporate world where some boundaries are virtual or collapsing and where global and local identities are being renegotiated. They consider that openness to others and a genuine interest in others are core attributes for leaders who are good at operating in a multicultural, globalised world. Otherness or difference is not seen as a problem or source of threat, but often as an opportunity for personal growth, for intellectual challenge, for professional expansion. This openness rests on a fairly confident identity, a source of identity not undermined when confronted by other ways of doing things. People who have this openness seem to have a balanced or moderate ego, robust enough to withstand and grow from challenge but not so inflated that the self can't step aside, appreciate and promote others. While they often have good people skills and empathy, their sense of identity is not defined by membership of a group. This finding connects to a distinction made by Zaleznik (1977) in early work distinguishing leaders from managers. Zaleznik argued that, based on their formative experiences, managers felt fundamentally more comfortable being part of a group – and were often lost without their group – while leaders were more solitary types.

Capabilities and strategies

(a) Reflecting on your role

The importance of reflectiveness in leadership has long been recognised by scholars. In 1978 Argyris and Schon identified the capacity, indeed the habit, of critically reflecting on one's actions and comments, of assessing and taking responsibility for consequences, and of learning from this process about alternative future actions as critical elements in leadership.

Most CEOs that Sinclair and Wilson interviewed visibly warmed to the opportunity the research provided to reflect on their own experiences and to draw insights about these experiences:

> I haven't been this reflective for a long time. You don't get the chance to be reflective as much as you'd like. I don't in my lifestyle.

In one sense, the fact that they were interested in the research and agreed to participate was a barometer of openness to reflection.

(b) Taking risks and testing self

Successful leadership in the radically transformed organisational landscape requires individuals, and organisations, to do unconventional things, make controversial appointments, adopt unpopular practices and tackle issues that other organisations may avoid. Personal shortcomings may need to be confronted, risks taken, mistakes made and owned up to. Sinclair and Wilson found that another feature of effective leadership was courage and a willingness to challenge accepted practices. Courage, coupled with the capacity to reflect and learn from mistakes, emerged as part and parcel of the adaptability many interviewees displayed.

The leaders also placed great personal value on learning, openness and maintaining interest beyond their business. Some had an enormous appetite for the new. Reviewing their careers, all had been willing to put themselves in different situations and see what happened. From this basic predisposition, there was evidence of a range of risk-taking styles – ranging from fairly calculating, planned and careful adoption of new roles (often in overseas countries) to, at the other extreme, a constant desire to test oneself against new challenges. Said one: " as soon as I get into a comfort zone, I find another cliff to jump off." Those "cliffs" might take the form of relatively minor forays into new or potentially uncomfortable areas of business or social situations, or it might be a major change of direction. Courage comes in many shapes and sizes:

> When I was at school I worked at a drop-in centre where we aligned ourselves with the dropouts of society. I'm on the World Vision Board now. I could spend my life working for them . . . It is very important for me . . . I feel a bit constrained now this has become a public company and I'm actually turning it into a company that's probably shortly not going to be the style of company I want to run. But I've fixed it. I like that. I don't want infinite continuity . . . I want new starts . . .

In the next example we see courage in the necessity to reach out to others, to put others at ease, even when you are the outsider.

> My experience in London really taught me a lot, it was a chance to immerse myself in a totally different environment . . . alone, no friend. Like all very big cities it was in that sense very cold . . . It took me a while to realise that wherever you are you've got to go out of your way to be friendly, you've got to take the first step . . . take the trouble to make a friendly gesture . . . if you wait for things to happen they probably won't.

(c) Negotiating outcomes

Leaders interviewed tended to reject the command and control approach to management as less successful in achieving objectives, preferring to negotiate outcomes and develop a sense of team ownership:

> I think my people-management skills and my communication ability (it sounds like I'm beating my own drum here) were definitely at a higher level than my peer group . . . just the ability to manage relationships, toward achieving a goal. I'm a very active negotiator, not in a formal sense, but I'll try and negotiate outcomes just through conversation and get people to see my point of view and I think this helps in an organisation.

(d) Working with all organisational levels

The histories of the leaders that were interviewed meant that they were as likely to identify with those at the bottom of the organisation as at the top. They were intolerant of badges of status and often more comfortable moving at lower levels of the organisation:

> I really enjoyed working with working-class people. Straightforward, no bullshit. I liked the physicality of the work. I enjoyed the skills I was learning. I loved having the skills of truck driving and forklift operation . . .I enjoyed being a rebel as well. Even in those days, I'd be at a old school reunion. "what do you do? "Oh I am a truck driver" I enjoyed that.

Another CEO described how listening to the concerns of the shopfloor, which had never been done before, delivered a complete change of organisational culture:

> My approach is to go there, spend a lot of time on the factory floor. I'm an engineer, I love factories! I can identify with what they do. We have some of the lowest award paid staff in Victoria – it's a regional country town, but we're the only major employer. You need to ask, 'What is the pain here? What is the anxiety? What do the workers want?' Discover the hot button – 'If I can't work who's going to look after my family?' So I asked the super fund how can we look after our staff if they can't work. Can we insure the whole workforce? It's never been done before. Got their rate down to 1 per cent. Go back and tell them as part of the enterprise bargaining negotiations we've now covered you . . . just forget about the tensions, it was all done. If you can identify with the pain, with the anxiety . . . it might cost 1 per cent of salary but for them it's a huge psychological boost . . . It repositioned the company's relationship with the employees overnight. It became a caring, understanding employer rather than adversarial.

(e) Challenging the status-quo

The leaders were willing to challenge the ways things had always been done. One CEO described two earlier employers, both with traditional managerial cultures as evidenced by status rituals such as reverence for an overseas head office, chauffers, silver service lunches and gardeners to maintain the rose garden. When he was recruited as local managing director, among his earliest actions was pulling out hundreds of roses and selling them to a local nursery. He was labelled 'a philistine, uncultured, I sold the silverware'. But as he describes it:

> I was not brought in to preserve a British hangover culture. This is a new world out there. We are a company not a nursery! I know they're beautiful but I don't want to spend time and money on pruning roses . . . I expanded our factories, made us a larger local content factory rather than an importer . . . It was almost like a cheek . . . I'm different . . . I'm a bit counter-establishment. That's why I disliked [previous organisation], everything so polished and perfect, there was nowhere for my creativity to apply itself . . . I don't copy.

(f) Listening to others

This is not merely a physical or mechanistic listening. It is active listening and those who are good at it seem to have the ability to get into the skin of the other person, if only momentarily:

> People come in here with huge problems for them, their conflicts with supervisors, with the system or policies. You've just got to find your way through these things. Sometimes when you sit and take time to talk to individuals you realise the capabilities they've got and how dismissive you can be because you don't know people or because you've got preconceived notions about their status or contribution.

RESEARCH QUESTION

Investigating a group of New Zealand leaders: their roots of, routes to, and routines in leadership.

Objectives
1. investigate their roots of leadership: family of origin, birth order, family size, relationship with parents
2. investigate their routes to leadership: pathways, and the significance of mentoring and training.
3. investigate their routines in leadership: daily activities of the leader
4. investigate whether the results are similar to those discovered by Sinclair and Wilson (2002) as outlined in *New Faces of Leadership*.

METHODOLOGY

This section of the report provides further support for the use of qualitative methods in researching leadership, and outlines the process used in this particular project.

Bryman and Stephens (1996) have suggested that a number of examples of research can be cited as illustrations of a qualitative research approach within leadership studies. Some of the popular books on leadership, such as Bennis and Nanus (1985), have employed interviews and informal observation to examine the strategies of successful, senior leaders, and have etched out the role of such features as "vision" to the leaders success. Roberts (1985) used a mixture of qualitative interviewing and observation to study a school superintendent in a Midwestern school district and the process by which she handled a budgetary crisis with which she was confronted by transforming the district. Tierney (1989) conducted semi-structured interviews with 32 presidents of U.S. colleges to determine the use of symbols in their leadership. This research showed how leader's symbolic messages may be more equivocal than is often realised. In a study of three British construction projects by Bryman et al. (1988), semi-structured interviews were employed to examine the influences on the approaches to leadership of construction site leaders. They show how features specific to the particular context of construction projects (such as project time urgency and the presence of subcontractors) have a profound effect on leadership behaviour. Pettigrew and Whipp's (1991) research used semi-structured interviews, observation and examination of documents to explore the process of leading change in eight organisations in four British industrial sectors. The context-sensitive and complex nature of the processes involved are highlighted by their study. Alvesson (1992) used a similar combination of methods in a study of the social integrative aspects of leadership in a computer consultancy company. Kirby et al. (1992) asked 58 graduate students to provide narratives to describe examples of "extraordinary leadership" that they had encountered . Writers in the field of strategic management, like Greiner and Bhambri (1989) and Gioia and Chittipeddi (1991), have carried out detailed qualitative case studies of the initiation of strategic change by incoming chief executive officers. These various studies are illustrative of the growing interest in and use of qualitative research in leadership studies.

Four different kinds of qualitative research design can be discerned in these various reports. First, there is the detailed case study of a single organisation and leader (Alvesson, 1992; Gioia & Chittipeddi, 1991; Roberts, 1985). This type of investigation usually employs participant observation, some semi-structured interviewing, and examination of documents, such as minutes of meetings and mission statements. Second, there is the multiple-case-study design in which there are detailed examinations of leaders in a small number of organisations (Bryman et al., 1988; Pettigrew & Whipp, 1991). This design usually aims to make direct comparisons between cases as a means of generating theoretical insights (Eisenhardt, 1989) and data are based largely on semi-structured interviews with the focal leaders and other key actors, along with the examination of relevant documents and a limited amount of participant observation. Third, there is the design that concentrates on what a fairly large number of leaders say about their leadership practices and orientations which is usually based on semi-structured interviews with the leaders concerned (Bennis and Nanus, 1985; Tierney, 1989). Finally, there is a design which invites people to describe in detail specific leaders or leadership practices in general (Kirby et al., 1992).

The methodology in this project most closely aligns with the third kind described above. It was modelled on that used by Sinclair and Wilson (2002) as outlined in the appendix of *New Faces of Leadership*. Modelled rather than replicated, in that although they had previously criticised the fact that most research into leadership concentrated on business leaders, they in fact chose to interview only business leaders. They described their process as:

We believed that real attitudes . . . would not be readily or usefully captured by large sample, questionnaire-type data gathering. . . . Our project methodology was therefore qualitative. The plan was to conduct discursive, narrative interviews to explore ideas about leadership.

Drawing on research, we developed an outline of the interview schedule. This was used as a prompt and to ensure that we covered all the areas we were interested in. But we were also very committed to, and experienced in, following the interviewees' narratives, 'hearing' in the fullest sense their experiences, and probing their most salient experiences and ideas . . . The interview schedule was a checklist rather than a map for the interview a we found that interviewees pursued their own unique course while covering the territory in which we were interested.

We conducted roughly half the interviews each, immediately doing a full verbatim transcript of our respective interviews of our respective interviews . . . The process of doing one's own verbatim transcripts is in itself a powerful research tool. It requires that one re-live the interview in a particularly painstaking and time-consuming way, poring over each word in the tape-recording, hearing once again not just the words, but the language, tone, nuance, hesitation, silence and so on.

My research was conducted with 5 leaders: one each from the church, school, business, sports, and public sectors, in an attempt to gain a broad spectrum of leadership backgrounds and practices. The project methodology was qualitative. I sought to conduct discursive, narrative interviews to explore: their roots of leadership (family of origin), their routes to leadership (pathways and mentoring), and what I have chosen to call, their routines in leadership (daily activities). The leaders were interviewed monthly, for approximately 30 minutes, over a 4-5 month period. The interviews were be taped and then transcribed by the researcher. The data collected was then evaluated for findings about the nature of leadership.

Following is an outline of the interview schedule. This was used as a prompt and to ensure that I covered all the areas I was interested in. But again, as above, I was very committed to following the interviewee's narrative – 'hearing' them, rather than directing them.

Meeting 1 - Introductions

Tell me a little about yourself – your gender, age, ethnicity, marital state, hobbies and interests.

Tell me about your current leadership role – staff reporting to you, your accountabilities etc,

Do you have any leadership roles outside your current one?

Meeting 2 – Roots of leadership

Tell me about you family of origin.

Tell me about your relationship with your mother and father.

Tell me about your place in the family and your siblings.

Meeting 3 – Routes to leadership

Tell me about your pathway into leadership.

Tell me about any experience of mentoring you have had.

Tell me about any training for leadership you have had.

Meeting 4 – Routines in leadership

Tell me about daily leadership activities.

Tell me about how you lead your followers.

Tell me how you see leadership differing from management.

The nature of interviews reflects the distinction Fontana and Frey (2000) made between the structured and the unstructured interview. The former aims at capturing precise data of a codable nature in order to explain behaviour within pre-established categories, whereas the latter attempts to understand complex behaviour of members of society without imposing any a priori categorisation that may limit the field of inquiry. The schedule follows their suggested pattern, in which, the researcher is involved an informal conversation with the respondent, and thus maintains the tone of a "friendly" chat while trying to remain close to the guideline of the topic of inquiry they have in mind. The researcher begins by "breaking the ice" with general questions and gradually moves onto more specific ones.

RESULTS

This section of the report contains the results of my interviews with the group of leaders, being a summary of each interview transcript.

Introductions

The sports leader interviewed is a 32 year old male, who works as a business adviser in the Immigration Service. Married with children, he has a Pakeha father and a Maori/Samoan mother. He has coached teams in both rugby and league for the last 4 years, and is currently coaching a Senior A league team. This takes up about 7 hours a week. He is also a deacon at the church he attends, a role he has had for the last 7 years.

The church leader interviewed is a 52 year old male, who works as the senior pastor of a Baptist church in Auckland. Married with children, he is a Pakeha and a fourth generation Kiwi. He is responsible for 2 other paid pastoral staff, and 3 voluntary pastoral staff and accountable to the church membership and an eldership board. For the last 5 years he has also been on the Assembly Council, which is the standing committee of the Baptist churches of New Zealand.

The public sector leader is a 49 year old male, who works as the area manager of a crown commission. His 22 staff manage the contracts of tertiary education providers in the area. Born in Britain his family migrated to New Zealand when he was 11 years old, and he is married with children. He is also on the board of a North Shore mental health provider and is the past has led the youth group at his church. He is accountable to the Auckland regional manger of the commission.

The school leader is a 49 year old female, who is the principal of a primary school with 275 pupils, 13 teachers and 5 aides. She has a Maori father and a Pakeha mother, and is married with children. She is also chairperson of the management group for the West Auckland cluster of resource teachers for learning and behaviour. She has been a principal for 7 years, which takes up most of her time. In the past she has served as an elder in the church she attended.

The business leader is a 46 year old male, who is the Chief Operations Officer for a telecommunications software company. He has 8 direct reports, and a functional relationship with 4 overseas staff in France and the United Kingdom. He is married with children, a Pakeha Kiwi with an English father and Kiwi mother. The family home is in Auckland but he commutes to work in Hamilton, which leaves little time for anything else, although in the past he was a deacon in the church he attends.

Roots of Leadership

The sports leader interviewed grew up in Devonport and from the age of 7 was raised by his father after his parents separated. His father had previously worked in a variety of jobs such as a storeman.

> My parents separated when I was about 7, until then my old man worked a variety of jobs such as a storeman and farmhand, but from that time he became a full time parent and beneficiary. He looked after us and raised us and did a little part-time work until he remarried which was after I had left home.

Although his father was the primary caregiver, he also lived with his mother at times. He got on well with both parents, although had issues with the fact that his mother had chosen to leave the family.

> But I attribute a lot to my old man because he did his best to raise us, and back in those days, the 70s and 80s, being a solo Dad wasn't really heard of. I get on well with my mother although we did have issues which probably arise from the fact that she is a strong willed character. But she left us and that had some effect. We would go and live with her and when she'd had enough we would be sent back to Dad. Quite tumultus during my teen years.

He is the second oldest, having an older brother and two younger siblings.

The church leader interviewed grew up In Morningside. His father worked as a meat truck driver, and his mother cared for the family as well as her own parents who lived in the same street.

> My recollection is growing up in Burnleigh Terrace, here in Auckland, Mum looked after the family, Dad worked as a meat truck driver, leaving home at 5am and returning at 5 or 6pm. He developed brucelocious, and arthritis, and had both hips done in his late 30s. He is up to his eighth hip replacement. My closest friends were a Tongan family up the road. There wasn't a lot of food, although always plenty of meat, perhaps because my Dad was a meat truck driver. This was 1952 and people were still recovering from the war, and my dad was still supporting his siblings. Mum was looking after her parents as well who ended up living with us.

He did not have a close emotional relationship with his parents as a child, due to them both being extremely busy, but formed a close bond with his maternal grandmother.

> My strongest emotional support was with my maternal grandmother who lived down the road from us. During my teenage years home was home but Grans was where I felt at home. Mum was busy looking after the home and when Dad came home he was exhausted from the physical labour. He was also in physical pain and would drink to dull it, Mum worried about this and joined him to show how bad it was but became more addicted than he. My parents were different people in the morning (nice) and evening (not nice).

He left home at 16 to go Police College. He is the second oldest, with an elder sister and two younger siblings.

The public sector leader interviewed grew up in England where his father was a regimental sergeant major in the Army.

> I was born in 1955, my father was a regimental sergeant-major in the Royal Engineers. So I grew up in a military setting. The expectation on the RSM was to look after the troops, also to be a role model and example, and I believe this came up especially when he was the RSM for the Dover Military Camp where young men aged 16 entered the army and did an induction before entering the regular army.

The family migrated to New Zealand when his father completed 25 years of service at age 39, and subsequently found work in engineering. His father was present through most of his youth and he would often accompany him on his rounds through the camp as his dealt with the troops.

> I think I lived in awe of my father because of what he did more than what he said. There was that role model of watching him deal with domestic issues among the troops, and when he was on base he would take me around with him. But I think my closest relationship was with my mother because she was there all the time, during my first 9 nine years, that was where the relationship was built and continues on to this day.

He saw his father as a role model but probably had a closer emotional relationship with his mother. His is the first -born and has a brother 9 years his junior.

The school leader interviewed grew up in west Auckland. Her mother worked for a company that supplied childcare and she attended this from the age of 3. Later her mother gave birth to a disabled child, care for which became her primary role.

> I grew up understanding that I was the eldest of 6 children. My father was Maori (Ngati Kahu) and had a traditionally Maori upbringing. My mother is European, from Wellington, she grew up until she was 15 as an only child, when her sister was born, and then another at 16. I have met me maternal grandmother three times in my life, all positive, I have never met my maternal grandfather who did not agree with mixed marriages. So my Mum virtually became disowned. My grandfather lived until my late 20s, I called him once and he was very polite, but I never met him.

From that time she often accompanied her father, her held multiple jobs such as lawn-mowing, and helped him with this work. She developed a close emotional tie with her father.

> I was probably closer to my Dad and was he companion from the time I was small because he absolutely enjoyed the company of kids, and was very relaxed about accommodating kids into his life. I always went with him when he went in the car, my mother would send me with him when he went to the rugby so he would come home

rather than go to the pub. So I would say he was really influential in my life, helping me set my value system.

She believed she was the eldest of 6 children until when aged 15 she discovered she had an older brother, and aged 40 an older sister, who had been adopted out. In her role as the evident oldest, and with her mother preoccupied, she was often responsible for much of the work of looking after her other siblings.

The business leader interviewed grew up in West Auckland, where his father owned a fruit and vegetable store that he had purchased at 51 after working many years as a truck driver.

> Dad came (to New Zealand) at 17 years old and never has returned. He has always worked 6 days a week in low paid jobs such as a truck driver, At 51 he cashed in his National Provident fund and bought a fruit and vegetable store in Railside Ave, Henderson. This was successful but later when he sold and bought another store in New Lynn he was caught in a price war with between similar stores at the same sight that ended up in the loss of his store and home, though not made bankrupt

His father always worked 6 days a week, busyness and tiredness not allowing for spending much time with his son. The family would holiday together every year, normally at Rotorua in holiday chalets owned by the Post Office for whom his mother worked when the children were of school age.

> I had a good relationship with my father but we never went fishing/camping as he worked 6 days a week. On Saturdays he would come home a go to sleep in his chair, tired out from the working week. However every Sunday however we went for a drive, either in the country or to places like the museum. We always went on family holidays, normally to Rotorua where the Post office had holiday homes. Mum was always home when I was growing up, to provide help.

He and his twin brother are the oldest of 6 children, though his twin is the eldest.

Routes to leadership

The sports leader found that during his playing career he was often selected as captain of teams he played in. Knowledge of his sporting involvement lead to him being approached to coach teams. He began on a trial and error basis but later attended a coaching clinic run by the Auckland Rugby Union (ARU).

> I don't think there was a structured pathway into what I am doing. When I used to play sport I used to end up in leadership positions, such as captain, I don't know if this was by virtue of being assertive on the paddock or in playing sport that I had a high work ethic about what I do. Having said that, getting into coaching sport, I started out coaching rugby. The members of the church team knew that I had played sport for many years and decided that I would be the best person to coach them. That by default got me into it, and by trail and error I learnt to put things together and off the cuff trying to run sessions. Eventually I did a coaching clinic with the Auckland Rugby Union which helped me put a structure to what I do in coaching.

He also has a friend who works in development for the ARU who has helped him with advise about coaching, showing him how to run sessions and pass on skills. He does not believe he has ever had a mentor but has drawn on his experience of being coached. The coach he felt he learned most from coached him in a sport, basketball, different from the sports, rugby – league and union, which he now coaches.

> I sort of have had a mentor in coaching, I guess I could relate it to, well not really, apart from coaches that I have had myself, and I haven't had any outstanding coaches. Although I did play basketball, and had a terrific coach when I captained the Unitec team for a couple of years. I thought he was a fantastic skills coach and was very particular with details and discipline, and that was very helpful. I also had a coach at high school who was very committed to fitness and discipline who taught me a lot.

He also tries to model himself on the example of well-known coaches, such as Graham Henry, adopting their practices such as extensive analysis. He does not read coaching books but rather sources information from the internet.

The church leader entered the Police at 16. He soon learnt that position didn't equate with leadership, observing that often squad sought direction from a member who did not hold the rank of sergeant. He went on to become a senior constable and watch-house keeper responsible for those held in the cells. He later transferred to the CIB and completed detective and sergeants exams.

> At 15.5 years I left home and joined the Police, which led to me becoming a cop and instantly you find yourself out and about and in situations, things you encountered on the street where you had to take charge. After being in the job a while you were the senior member and took control and gave directions to other staff, so there was that hands on, take charge, organise things, experience at a young age. Then as a senior constable I began to take more leadership, then I became the shift watch-house keeper which means that I took charge of the cells and getting prisoners to court, organise the staff and keep the records.

He resigned from the Police and went to theological college where part of his training was in pastoral leadership. He put this into practical application during summer assignments at churches, one of which, when their pastor had a nervous breakdown, requested that he pastor their church during his final year of study. He has observed and learnt from negative leadership models in both the Police and the church. He did not have anyone act as a mentor to him but has intentionally sought to connect with other leaders in ministry roles to speak into his life.

> Mentors along the way for me have been interesting. There weren't many in my time in the Police, there were those with rank but they tended to be inept and I didn't have time for. And in the church, no, there weren't people there who were mentors for me. At Faith BC and a Pentecostal church we attended in Wellington, I instead saw examples of spiritual abuse. When we left we went to a Baptist church and there I encountered a man who was a real pastor, gentle and a good shepherd. At the same time I intentionally tried to connect with people who were leaders in various roles and institutions, not especially seeking mentors, but they did speak into my life, and encouraged me to see myself as a leader. Not that I would be but that I was. So in discussion with people like that I started to sharpen my thinking about leadership.

An individual who was the denominational leader has become a mentor to him in recent years. He attended a church leadership course in 1998 which he found helpful in parts. He has recently completed a graduate research project on an appropriate model of pastoral leadership for a local church. He has read books on leadership by authors such as Covey (*7 Habits of Highly Effective People)* and Maxwell (*21 Laws of Leadership*) but believes that business models of leadership are not directly transferable to the church.

The public sector leader received leadership experience early on in the Scouts. In his first job he was asked to take over leadership of an office of three older men due to his technical expertise and higher qualifications.

> I think it actually started for me, probably with opportunities given to me in groups like Scouts in the old days, but I think when I started my working life it was around mastery of the particular job, a series of projects which I had, I was thinking of my first job after I left university where I was offered the opportunity to come up to Auckland to take over an office where there were 3 older guys mainly because I had a reputation of being a good technical draughtsman and also the most highly qualified of the 4, that was probably my first opportunity to take leadership in a workplace.

Through personal connections this led to the opportunity to lead a group of 120 volunteers working on a kibbutz in Israel. Returning to New Zealand he began working in a government department where he was asked to lead a team of older, more experienced men. He felt it was important that he establish credibility before mastery. To achieve the latter he sought out mentors who give him knowledge and direction. He also undertook departmental training in leadership through short courses and seminars. He also values external mentors who serve as a reality check on what he is doing.

> There were a number of programs I took in training for leadership, some quite short courses, some I did through external organisations and some I did through Corrections. Through discussions with mentors I could ask where I could get training for the skills I lacked or whether I should give up on them and find someone else who had them, that is the way I tried to build this office, saying what are the skills we've got, where could we get complementary skills.

He believes it is important to recognise your own skills and seek to supplement personal deficiencies by building a team around him who are skilled in areas he is not.

The school leader being the eldest of 6 children, of whom the second by being disabled took the bulk of her mother's time, had from her early years to exercise leadership in the family by looking after her siblings. In her early teens she became part of a church youth group where she filled leadership positions and received leadership training.

> As a young person I was very involved in my church youth group, and I think people saw leadership qualities in me from way back and so I would really give a lot of credit to those people, because these are the people that invested a lot of time and effort to develop leadership abilities in my life, and they did that by having us work on youth committees and giving us the skills to break down tasks, looking at whole pictures, looking at goals, looking at vision, from quite an early age, from 12 or 13. People like that who stuck with me, even helping me determine what were my options, coming from a lower socio-economic area, having to leave home at 16, what educational and life options were out there for a person like me, being a young Maori woman.

Two leaders of this group, who were also church elders and teachers, became life-long mentors and friends. They encouraged her to complete her education and train as a teacher.

> They were mainly men, both youth group leaders and elders, about every second one happened to be involved in education, and I think they also believed that education made a difference in peoples lives. When I look back there were 2 key people (RE & BH). They became leaders, mentors and ultimately friends. I would still be able to approach those 2 people for help about any issue. They were the type of men who you could trust to know all your good, all your bad, all your potential and give you an honest appraisal.

In her early teaching she specialised in at-risk youth. After an OE, marriage and children, she returned to teaching and soon moved to Special Education Services where she was responsible for all at-risk Maori students in West Auckland. Later she returned to teaching and was soon shoulder tapped for assistant principal and then principal of the school. As soon as she got this position she began attending every seminar or course she could on leadership and time-management and utilising presenters as mentors.

The business leader never set out to become one, but there came a time when he decided he didn't want to remain "just one of the troops, sat back in the trenches, being told what to do." He thus chose to move from the technical (field) group to the middle (office) group. He took initiative and became the manager's right hand man, fulfilling his responsibilities when he was absent.

> After we moved to Auckland I had the opportunity to apply for a position in what was then Telecom, which was a management role, and to my surprise, and everyone else, I got it. But I think that was part of having already displayed initiative. I was part of an engineering group, and I assumed the unofficial, unpaid role of being the right hand man to the manager of that group, so I started doing it, when he was away of leave I would assume some of his duties, and no-one recognised me as the manager, though they kind of did unofficially, there was no conflict. So I had been doing it unofficially before I applied for the job.

He then applied for a management job (he notes that in business you apply for management jobs rather than leadership jobs) and got it. He found that he enjoyed the work and seems to possess the skills to lead others. He did go back to university and complete a Diploma in Business Studies but felt this was more to acquire technical skills.

> In terms of formal education, I raced off to Auckland Uni and did a Diploma In Business Studies but that was more about management and the technical skills needed. I picked strategic management because that was my background but that really wasn't leadership training, but good leadership involves having a range of those skills, and to be able to demonstrate to other people that you know what you are talking about, its all part of the mix, but no I have never done any formal leadership training.

For him, you are either a leader or you are not, he has worked with managers who have the title but are not leaders. Although technical knowledge is important he now leads a team of software engineers although having no expertise in that field. He has read some business books but finds them hard, he never got past the foreword of his copy of Tom Peters *Thriving on Chaos,* and prefers shorter articles from magazines which deal with current and past leaders, such as Lester Levy. He believes that the key step to leadership is that opportunity to your first management position, denied that people may not become a recognised leader.

Routines in leadership

The sports leader felt that the key activity of leadership was being clear strategically about where you are going and then communicating those decisions to the team.

> It is a lot about preparation and forward planning, so before a season starts you have to be thinking about goals and what things need to happen so getting players fit and teaching technique and then when you get to winter it is about how to keep them motivated and so providing variation to training and also on a routine basis you have to look analytically at what you are doing so that involves things like statistics, analysing your game and seeing what your deficiencies are and player management. So you are thinking about injury and how to manage injury, and you are thinking about form and selection and those sorts of things.

This necessitated a lot of preparation and forward planning to clarify goals and determine what things the team had to do individually and corporately to achieve them. He also felt that leadership involved setting an example of how to behave, so required being on time for practices and maintaining personal fitness.

> I probably don't motivate people by speech it is more about what you do, but for me it is about being that example. It is about having everything set out for them so that they know where they are going and they are objective because you are objective.

He felt that the team expected the coach to be up-to-date with technical knowledge and show that he knew what he was talking about. He chose to motivate people by example rather than by speech.

The church leader saw the Sunday service as his key activity in which he had the opportunity to nurture and encourage and even model the behaviour which he wishes the congregation adopt.

> Leadership for a pastor is an iterative process, because it is not just the institution, but it is also those services and activities of the church ministries – I don't see the service as being ancillary but central, in the sense that I see worship as being pastoral care, not of the individual but of the group. It is trying to feed that stuff which is central to the core, central to the goals, aims, all those things which we wish to hold. So on a Sunday service we have an opportunity to nurture and encourage, to even model how you want those thing s to happen.

He leads the congregation by helping them to become what they are supposed to be – to help them reach their full potential, rather than using them as units of production to meet the minister's goals.   This involves encouraging and resourcing them to exercise their individual ministry within the congregation as a whole.

> My jobs is about 3 things, the first is leading the congregation – helping them to be what they are supposed to be, I said in my application that I saw my role as comforting the afflicted and afflicting the comforted, so you must be constantly challenging people or meeting them at their point of challenge, to keep them focussed and moving in the right direction. The second thing is caring for the people concerned, both inside and outside the church in ways that are practical and helpful, not doing for them what they should be for themselves, but encouraging and resourcing them. The third thing is, because this is not just a group of people who gather together voluntarily for a picnic but an organisation that has a budget and staff, and I have to manage that part as well.

The model for Christian leadership is set out in Donald McGraven's *The Upside-down Kingdom*, which emphasises that leadership in a Christian setting is about service. So the way to demonstrate leadership is by serving the people. By serving and preaching the leader keeps in front of people the big picture of the role of the church corporate and the Christian individual.

The public sector leader saw his main activity as "thinking outside the square". He felt that while managers work within the square, the leader must think outside the square. Strategic thinking requires that the leader examines all possibilities, even dream the dreams of what might be possible, and then review the implications of those possibilities.

> I think there is firstly a clear delineation between management/administration and leadership. One of them is about thinking in the square and one of them is thinking outside the square. If I can make an example of thinking in the square is about following the policies in terms of making sure they are kept to the quality and the consistency that is desired, making sure all the boxes are ticked and making sure all the processes are followed. Leadership takes it to the next stage further and says what are the implications of these decisions, where might this lead to, what are the sort of things that I need to communicate to the staff in terms of the possibilities and then taking an active role in terms of taking the management to the next level.

He then has to take the initiative to implement the chosen possibility, informing and enthusing his team about how they can be part of achieving the dream. Thus leadership is about developing people to reach their potential, to encourage them to step outside their comfort zone and test their self-imposed limitations.

> Part of it is in terms of the approach is that I am here to enable other people to do their best and part of that is I think from my prospective is trying to keep a sense of humility. Yes I did have the best idea and yes it might do this however try to let someone else take the credit for it. So it is about looking at those possibilities. Leaders do not go out on their own because forms of leadership I think are fairly arrogant in terms of this is what we are going to do and this is where we are going I will tell you what to do. Part of leadership is about development of people.

The leader must inspire confidence in his people by demonstrating a knowledge of where things are going, displaying calm and directing people back to the objective when they are distracted by other issues.

The school leader felt her key activity was about having the big picture of where the school was going, of having done the creative thinking before anyone else so that she knows the pros and cons of what may be suggested.

Leadership for me in this position is about me having the big picture and the difference about having the big picture which impacts on management decisions is that when people come with a budget want or whatever, or even if they want something really impactful in terms of ICT, my job is to be able to have the big picture which may be a 3-5 year plan as to where we are going and I would think that I would have had to have done that creative thinking before anyone else sometimes so that I know all the pros and cons to what they are asking. If I haven't done the thinking then my job is to go and do that – but if I have the big picture so I can direct people so that it slots in, in the right time frame and time line, so I see that as really important and it is a big picture across the board virtually about everything about the institution I am leading.

To assist her to do that, she saw her participation in professional development through courses or conferences as essential. She also felt it was important to find out how people feels they fit into the picture and what they want to do, and then to empower them to achieve those goals. Sometimes this involves seeing the potential in people before they recognise it themselves and steering them appropriately.

The other part of professional development is about growing people who I work with or people or perceive me as their leader or boss. I think that is a huge challenge. I think my job is to find out what they want to do and then empower them to get to what they want to do, which may mean (and this has happened to me heaps of times) where I train someone up the way I want to and then of course they need to move on, it would be much easier for me to keep them but of course it is about their personal growth, so it is thinking all the time about that. For me too a huge part of my leadership job, I think it is linked into my gifting, is about the potential I see in people, so I am always scanning when I see courses or professional development I think 'oh so and so is interested in this and we have talked about him maybe pursuing more of this and this may be the course for them' and running this past them or saying have you thought about this and so I think that is where leadership differs from day to day management.

She feels that a leader must be a risk-taker, but a calculated risk-taker, who thinks outside the square, not allowing themselves to be limited by present resources or approaches. The leader is freer to do this when they can deputize the day-to-day management activities.

The business leader saw his key activity as ensuring that all his staff have something useful to do, and weren't sitting around wondering where their next project was coming from. Good utilisation of people requires that he is very clear about what the end goal of each project is, and is able to communicate to his staff the role they have in reaching that goal. It is about keeping "everyone on the same page," communicating how well the team is doing at meeting the target, identifying where extra effort may be required, and who could do with assistance from others:

> It's the longer term view, it's about keeping everyone on the same page. We have a weekly morning tea, where the company buys the morning tea, and we take a bit longer, in a informal/semi-formal way to talk about how well coming is doing or not doing. You know, "hey guys we are a little bit behind on delivering on some of these projects, and finance needs 3 completed by the end of this month, so its going to be really busy this week." So there's a little bit of management but also a little bit of leadership. "We are all going to have to dig a little bit deeper this week, if we do the company is looking good, if we miss the cash flow will be poor next month, and the wages bill will be tight." So we share those issues, so everyone knows how they need to do their bit but also be ready to help others. This communicates to staff that they are involved in something greater than their day-to-day duties.

He also sees people development as an important role. He tries to talk regularly to people about what they want to do and where they see the next opportunities for career development..

> But leadership activities are all about, what I consciously try to do is talk to people about what they want to do, about their career aspirations, about where they see the next opportunities. That's important because people need to feel that they are coming to work to do a job, but that it is leading somewhere, otherwise I think it all becomes a bit pointless and meaningless.

DISCUSSION

This section of the report considers how the material in Results relates to other research findings, especially those of Sinclair and Wilson (2002).

Roots of leadership

Sinclair and Wilson found that more than half of their leaders had grown up without strong father identification. The result was not as clear in my findings.

One leader never had a strong relationship with his father:

> My father and I never saw eye to eye and it seemed to me that he never cared who I was or what I did or he wanted to argue about it. But I am grateful for my Gran and the Dad of a friend who became like an uncle, who gave me the opportunity to speak and vent, and negotiate some difficult years.

Pre-occupation with work prevented two leaders from having as deep a relationship as they would have liked:

> I had a good relationship with my father but we never went fishing/camping as he worked 6 days a week. On Saturdays he would come home a go to sleep in his chair, tired out from the working week.

> I think I lived in awe of my father because of what he did more than what he said. There was that role model of watching him deal with domestic issues among the troops, and when he was on base he would take me around with him. But I think my closest relationship was with my mother because she was there all the time, during my first 9 nine years, that was where the relationship was built and continues on to this day.

For one leader his father was the principal caregiver:

> My parents separated when I was about 7, until then my old man worked a variety of jobs such as a storeman and farmhand, but from that time he became a full time

parent and beneficiary. He looked after us and raised us and did a little part-time work until he remarried which was after I had left home.

The leader who had the closest relationship with their father was the only female leader interviewed:

I was probably closer to my Dad and was his companion from the time I was small because he absolutely enjoyed the company of kids, and was very relaxed about accommodating kids into his life. I always went with him when he went in the car, my mother would send me with him when he went to the rugby so he would come home rather than go to the pub. So I would say he was really influential in my life, helping me set my value system.

The male leaders reported stronger emotional links with their mothers. This, with the evidence of not as strong a connection with their fathers as desired, aligns well with other findings. For example Kets de Vries (2004):

There is evidence that many successful male leaders had strong supportive mothers and rather remote, absent fathers. This is beautifully exemplified by Jack Welch, who, in his autobiography, describes his attachment to a powerhouse of a mother and depicts his father, a train conductor, as pleasant enough but not very present. The same was true of a very different leader – Virgin's Richard Branson, whose mother told everyone she knew that Richard would one day become prime-minister. It was Branson's mother who convinced him that he could do whatever he set his mind to; his father played a much smaller role in his life.

Sinclair and Wilson also found that their leaders came from larger families and generally were not the eldest child.

The result of my research was the same for family size. Two leaders came from families with six children. Two came from families with four children. The other leader was one of two children.

However in relation to birth-order my findings aligned more with traditional findings that show a preponderance of first-born children among leaders. Three of the five leaders were first-born, and the other two were the second child in their family. Mant (1997) noted:

> Leading from the front is, metaphorically speaking, the province of the first-born child. Leading from behind is the younger siblings speciality. The psychologist Alfred Alder described the first born as characteristically a *'power-hungry conservative'* . . . It is no coincidence that the executive suites of public and private-sector organisations all around the world are peopled by so many first-borns.

Sinclair and Wilson noted that several of their interviewees had changed countries, exposing them to foreignness and difference, which created the need for adaptability.

This was the case for one leader in his youth:

> My father entered the military at 14 and left after 25 years at 39 at which time the whole family migrated to NZ. And we came out to NZ as a pod leaving behind all our relations in the UK to forge a new life.

Another leader had followed the more traditional 'Kiwi OE' experience:

> I taught for about 4 years, went overseas, did some life training, got married, came back, had our first baby and then went back to day to day relieving, which I had done in the States too.

Another leader had recently returned form the United Kingdom where he had spent two years as the representative of a New Zealand company.

Routes to leadership

Sinclair and Wilson found that more than half of the leaders that they interviewed had arrived in their present position from quite different fields.

This was also the case for the majority of leaders I interviewed. The church leader came from the Police. The public sector leader had worked for Probation but now was working in Education. The business leader had worked as engineer for Telecom but was now managing a software company. The sports leader had played basketball but ended up coaching rugby.

The school leader was the only one who had stayed in the same field, yet she conformed to Sinclair and Wilson's finding that such people had often worked in a different department of the organisation:

> I then went to Special Education where I was responsible for all at risk Maori students, from pre-school to high school, in west Auckland, one person.

Sinclair and Wilson found that a number of leaders commented on the assistance of a mentor in their career, although in most cases it was good advice at the right time, rather than sustained support.

Among the leaders I interviewed only the school leader was mentored for a sustained period, and in her case those involved were more like life-mentors rather than job mentors:

> When I look back there were 2 key people (RE & BH). They became leaders, mentors and ultimately friends. I would still be able to approach those 2 people for help about any issue. They were the type of men who you could trust to know all your good, all your bad, all your potential and give you an honest appraisal.

Two of the other leaders (public service and church) valued input from mentors but found that they had to seek them out themselves:

> Another opportunity came when I started at Probation, where I was given the opportunity to lead teams of older men who knew lots more than me, which was less about gaining mastery in the job and more about gaining credibility in their eyes. Here I benefited from mentors who I actively sort to give me advice and kick me when I needed it and then gradually obtain mastery.

> Mentors along the way for me have been interesting. There weren't many in my time in the Police, there were those with rank but they tended to be inept and I didn't have time for. And in the church, no, there weren't people there who were mentors for me. At Bible College and a Pentecostal church we attended in Wellington, I instead saw examples of spiritual abuse. When we left we went to a Baptist church and there I encountered a man who was a real pastor, gentle and a good shepherd. At the same time I intentionally tried to connect with people who were leaders in various roles and

institutions, not especially seeking mentors, but they did speak into my life, and encouraged me to see myself as a leader.

The others (business and sport) felt that they had never had a mentor but rather seen leadership modelled:

> I saw leadership modelled in other people, but no I have never had a mentor as such, I have never sat alongside anyone, I really have done it on my own. I have seen what I regard as great managers and leaders and I have seen some pretty ordinary ones, you know what behaviours to avoid and what behaviours to model.

> I sort of have had a mentor in coaching, I guess I could relate it to, well not really, apart from coaches that I have had myself, and I haven't had any outstanding coaches.

It is doubtful whether the relationships described by Sinclair and Wilson's interviewees, or those described by mine, conform to the common understanding of mentoring, a definition of which is supplied by Bowen (1986)

> Mentoring occurs when a senior person (mentor) in terms of age and experience undertakes to provide information, advice, and emotional support to a junior person (protégé) in a relationship lasting over an extended period of time and marked by substantial emotional commitment by both parties. If opportunity presents itself, the mentor uses both formal and informal forms of influence to further the career of the protégé.

Training-for-leadership was not addressed by Sinclair and Wilson in their research. My finding was that all of the leaders interviewed engaged in leadership training after their appointment to a position of leadership, but had not specifically undertaken training prior to that point, although the church leader had received some general training in the field of spiritual leadership during his denominational training. Most of the post-appointment training was of the shorter/seminar nature. Reading on leadership was done in like manner.

Although they had not engaged in formal leadership training prior to attaining the position, they all felt that they had been learning on the job. Cronin (1993) commenting on teaching leadership viewed this as the norm.

> Leadership study strikes me as an explicitly vocational topic. Its practical and applied matter – better learned in summer jobs, in internships or on the playing fields. You learn it by making mistakes and learning from these.

Involvement in church leadership activities, which was cited by all my interviewees probably arises from my selection process. I selected leaders I had been in contact with, and most of the contact arose from my experience in church circles in Auckland. However they all attend different local churches, within three different denominations.

Routines in leadership

The activity that was most commonly mentioned by the leaders was that of communicating the vision of their organisation and ensuring that their followers kept to it:

> There are all those regular meeting that you schedule, that are all about ensuring that the team is functioning together and that we are all heading in the same direction, sharing information, bouncing ideas of one another.

> I think the leaders job is to keep the big picture in front of the people and not get distracted by the other stuff.

> The principle is that management are getting the day-to-day things done in an effective and efficient way whereas leadership is about sharing a vision and taking people along.

> But I see leadership as mainly about 'hey look this is where we are going, this is my decision as to where we should be going as a team and providing them with I guess an example and a role model by providing good quality in the way that you coach.

> Leadership for me in this position is about me having the big picture and the difference about having the big picture which impacts on management decisions is that when people come with a budget want or whatever, or even if they want something really impactful in terms of ICT, my job is to be able to have the big picture which may be a 3-5 year plan as to where we are going.

To communicate a vision they had to have engaged in strategic thinking about the possibilities for their organisation:

> Leadership takes it to the next stage further and says what are the implications of these decisions, where might this lead to, what are the sort of things that I need to communicate to the staff in terms of the possibilities and then taking an active role in terms of taking the management to the next level.

> It is a lot about preparation and forward planning, so before a season starts you have to be thinking about goals and what things need to happen so getting players fit and teaching technique.

> If I haven't done the thinking then my job is to go and do that – but if I have the big picture so I can direct people so that it slots in, in the right time frame and time line, so I see that as really important and it is a big picture across the board virtually about everything about the institution I am leading.

> The number one for any project is to understand what the endpoint of the project is, what are the deliverables, and then you communicate that. If you are clears what the end goal is then the whole leadership thing sorts itself out.

The development of the people they lead was seen as an activity that had be undertaken to help achieve the vision and deliver the strategies.

> The other part of professional development is about growing people who I work with or people or perceive me as their leader or boss. I think that is a huge challenge. I think my job is to find out what they want to do and then empower them to get to what they want to do.

> Part of leadership is about development of people. It is about encouraging people to explore and try things to reach their potential. To do something outside their boundaries and test their limitations.

> The most effective that this church can work is for every member to be doing what they are supposed to be doing, and my job as the leader is to help them find out what their gift/ministry is, and then to encourage and resource them to do it efficiently.

> But leadership is about the people themselves, about adding flesh to the resource. It's the human part of the human resources.

Also the leaders often brought up activities that Sinclair and Wilson had identified in their section on capabilities and strategies.

(a) Reflecting on your role

As Sinclair and Wilson found, the leaders warmed to the opportunity the research afforded to reflect and draw insights from their experiences. Similarly they found that they did not get as much opportunity to spend time reflecting on their role as they would like. The church leader attempts to undertake a retreat each year to reflect, but even he found that the pressure of work often prevented this.

(b) Taking risks and testing self

Most of the leaders felt that taking risks was necessary to lead effectively:

> I think leadership to is different for maintenance because I think people would see me as a risk taker but I am a very calculated risk taker and I would have done a lot of pros and cons, what would I do if all the things went wrong, what would be my strategic back up plan if that happened, I think I do a lot of that stuff by myself but once I have checked off all my list of where could it go wrong, then I can move because I have done that.

> It is about taking a bit of a risk too, putting yourself out there and saying well OK I am prepared to be shot down

Sinclair and Wilson noted that their leaders often tested themselves by adopting new roles, sometimes in new countries.

This was common among the leaders I interviewed. Some had adopted new roles: from policemen to minister, from teacher to special education manager, from probation to tertiary education. The business leader had just returned from two years managing part of his company's activities in the United Kingdom.

(c) Negotiating outcomes

Sinclair and Wilson's leaders tended to reject the command and control approach preferring to negotiate outcomes and develop a sense of team ownership. This too was evident:

> We have a weekly morning tea, where the company buys the morning tea, and we take a bit longer, in a informal/semi-formal way to talk about how well coming is doing or not doing. You know, "hey guys we are a little bit behind on delivering on some of these projects, and finance needs 3 completed by the end of this month, so its going to be really busy this week."

(d) Working with all organisational levels

Like Sinclair and Wilson's leaders, they sought to be open to approaches from all staff and not restrict themselves to management.

> Generally when people arrive at work first thing in the morning they generally want to come and see me, so its just about being available for people to walk in and talk to me about projects.

> I try to say hello to everyone who comes past me and treat them like a person, connect with them about the last time I had a conversation with them, so if I need to check up

(e) Challenging the status-quo

"Thinking outside the square" was the most common response by interviewees to show that like Sinclair and Wilson's leaders they were not limited by the status-quo:

So that means I have to do the reading and mean that I go to conferences or lectures and things that maybe other people are not even thinking about right now, but there is a huge part of leadership which is about constantly thinking into the future.

I think there is firstly a clear delineation between management/administration and leadership. One of them is about thinking in the square and one of them is thinking outside the square.

(f) Listening to others

My interviewees valued this, as did Sinclair and Wilson's:

All the time you are touching base with people, asking whether they have any issues, any hassles. Because to me its all about dealing with issues as they come along, week by week, not leaving them and waiting for a big blow-up.

The routines in leadership discussed above relate closely to those outlined by Kouzes and Posner (1987). They saw core activities as:

- Challenging the process – This means searching for opportunities and experimenting, even taking sensible risks, to improve the organisation.
- Inspiring a shared vision – This is focussed less on inspiration per se and more on what leaders actually do to construct future visions and build follower support for the vision.
- Enabling others to act – Leaders make it possible for followers to take action by fostering collaboration (as opposed to competition) and supporting followers in their personal development.
- Modelling the way – Leaders set example by their own behaviours. They also help followers focus on step-by-step accomplishments of large-scale goals, making those goals seem more realistic and attainable
- Encouraging the heart – Leaders recognise follower's contributions and find ways to celebrate their achievements.

CONCLUSIONS

This section of the report concludes that qualitative research has an on-going role in investigating leadership, and reviews my findings and their place in that body of research.

Conger (1998) in arguing, "Why qualitative research must play a pivotal role in leadership studies," suggests that the main reason is the extreme and enduring complexity of the leadership phenomenon itself. For the foreseeable future, there will be no endpoint – a moment where researchers will be able to say we have now a complete and shared understanding of leadership. This is powerfully exemplified by the fact that after literally thousands of studies in the field we have yet to develop "a general theory of leadership that explains all aspects of the process adequately" (Yukl, 1994, p.19).

He further states, that as many of us are aware, this complexity is a by-product of several important characteristics of leadership. Specifically, leadership involves multiple levels of phenomena, possesses a dynamic character, and has a symbolic content.

These three dimensions of leadership – multiple levels, dynamism, and social construction – make for a very complex research topic. Conger (1998) asserts that as a result the subject ultimately demands multiple research methods – regardless of the field's stage of maturity. Quantitative research methods in and of themselves are insufficient of the grounds that they capture relatively uni-dimensional and static perspectives on leadership. On the other hand, qualitative methods offer the leadership field several distinct advantages over quantitative methods: (a) more opportunities to explore leadership phenomena in significant depth and to do so longitudinally (Bryman, 1992), (b) the flexibility to discern and detect unexpected phenomena during research (Lundberg, 1976), (c) an ability to investigate processes more effectively, (d) greater chances to explore and be sensitive to contextual factors, (e) and more effective means to investigate symbolic dimensions (Morgan & Smirich, 1980).

Conger's (1988) assertion about quantitative research's limitations matches my own experience in this research project. Having the desire to investigate leadership, my literature review initially made me feel that the approaches taken did not address the depth and breadth of leadership that I hoped to research. Then I came across Sinclair and Wilson's (2002) work that introduced me to the field of qualitative research of leadership. Here I felt I found a mechanism that provided for a richer approach to the investigation of leadership.

Thus my research project has been a qualitative investigation into the roots of leadership (family of origin), routes to leadership (mentoring and training), and routines in leadership (daily activities) for a group of New Zealand leaders.

The main limitation of the project was the small number of leaders interviewed – five, by comparison Sinclair and Wilson interviewed thirty. However it was not restricted, as they did, to only business leaders but involved leaders each from the church, sport, school, business and public sectors. The interviewees were from different ethnicities and included both genders.

In the roots of leadership section, I found that among the New Zealand leaders interviewed first-born sons were predominant. This outcome conforms to findings of research by Mant (1997) who investigated the relation between birth order and leadership. Secondly I found that the leaders interviewed tended to have a stronger emotional link with their mothers, and fathers who were otherwise occupied. This finding also is consistent with the results of similar research by Kets de Vries (2004). Lastly I found that the leaders who participated in the research came from large families with four to six children. Sinclair and Wilson (2002) found the same characteristic among leaders they interviewed in Australia.

In the routes to leadership section, I found that among the New Zealand leaders interviewed the majority had come to their present position from a different field of work. This was also the finding of research conducted by Sinclair and Wilson (2004) into the pathways of Australian leaders. The majority had also not experienced a mentoring relationship of the type Bowen (1986) had researched. Nor had they engaged in any specific leadership training prior to obtaining their position, but rather felt that they had learnt 'on-the-job', as Cronin (1993) expected most leaders would. However since entering a leadership role I found that they all undertook seminars and reading to improve their leadership understanding and skills.

In the routines in leadership section, I found that among the New Zealand leaders interviewed priority was given to communicating the vision of their organisation and ensuring that their followers kept to it. Strategic thinking and the development of the staff they led also were seen as key activities. These routines in leadership were congruent with the findings of Kouzes and Posner (1987) who investigated the core activities of leaders. Leaders I interviewed also referred to capabilities and strategies outlined in the findings that Sinclair and Wilson (2002) made about routine activities of Australian leaders.

As Conger (1998) states, it is unlikely that in the near future we will arrive at a moment where researchers will be able to say that we have now a complete and shared understanding of leadership. I therefore present my findings as a small contribution to the ongoing study of this rich and complex subject.

Further areas for research that could arise from my findings may include:
- Would the findings on the roots of leadership be the same across different ethnic groups in New Zealand?
- With the rise of leadership training courses in New Zealand, are the younger generation of leaders more likely to undertake training prior to obtaining a position of leadership?
- Is the communicating of vision influenced by the degree that the individual leader is involved in its creation?

REFERENCES

Alvesson, M. (1992). Leadership as social integrative action: a study of a computer consultancy company. *Organisational Studies,* 13, 185-209

Argyris, C. & Schon, D. (1978). *Organisational Learning: A Theory of Action Perspective."* Reading MS: Addison Wesley

Bass, B. (1990). *Bass and Stogdill's handbook of leadership: A survey of theory and research.* New York NY: Free Press

Bass, B (1985). *Leadership and performance based expectations.* New york NY: Free Press

Bennis, W. & Nanus, B. (1985). *Leaders: The Strategies of Taking Charge.* New York: Harper and Row

Blake, R & McCanse, A. (1991). *Leadership dilemmas – Grid solutions.* Houston TX: Gulf

Blake R. & Mouton, J. (1964). *The Managerial Grid.* Houston TX: Gulf

Blanchard, K., Zigarmi, P., & Zigarmi, D. (1985) *Leadership and the one-minute-manager: Increasing effectiveness through situational leadership.* New York: William Morrow

Bryman, A. (1992). *Charisma and leadership in organisations.* London: Sage

Bryman, A. & Stephens, M. (1996). The importance of context: Qualitative research and the study of leadership. *Leadership Quarterly* 7(3), 353-371

Bryman, A., Brensen, M., Beardsworth, A & Keil, T. (1988). Qualitative research and the study of human relationship. *Human Relations,* 41, 13-30

Cartwright, D. & Zander, A. (1960). *Group dynamics research and theory.* Evanston IL: Row, Peterson

Cronin, T. (1993). Reflections on Leadership. In Rosenbach, W. & Taylor, R. (Eds.) *Contemporary Issues in leadership.* Westview Press: Boulder

Conger, J. (1998). Qualitative research as the cornerstone methodology for understanding leadership. *Leadership Quarterly* 9(1), 107-21

Danserau, F., Graen, G. & Haga, W. (1975). A vertical dyad linkage approach to leadership in formal organisations. *Organisational Behaviour and Human Performance,* 13, 46-78

Dubrin, A. & Dalglish, C (2003). *Leadership: An Australasian focus,* Milton QLD: John Wiley & Sons

Evans, M. (1970). The effects of supervisory behaviour on the path-goal relationship. *Organisational Behaviour and Human Performance,* 5, 277-298

Eisenhardt, K. (1989). Building theories from case study research. *Academy of Management Review,* 14, 532-50

Fiedler, F. (1964). A contingency model of leadership effectiveness. In L. Berkowitz (Ed.), *Advances in experimental psychology* (Vol. 1, pp. 149-190)

Fiedler, F. & Chemers, M. (1974). *Leadership and effective management.* Glenview IL: Scott, Foresman

Fleishman, E., Mumford, M., Zaccaro, S., Levin, K., Korotkin, A. & Hein, M. (1991). Taxonomic efforts in the description of leader behaviour: A synthesis and functional interpretation. *Leadership Quarterly,* 2(4), 245-287

Fontana, A. & Frey, J. (2000). The interview: From structures questions to negotiated text. In N. Denzin & Y. Lincoln (Eds.) *Handbook of Qualitative Research* (2nd. Ed.) Thousand Oaks CA: Sage

Garner, H. (1984, 1993). *Frames of Mind: The Theory of Multiple Intelligences.* London: Fontana

Graen, G. (1976). Role-making processes within complex organisations. In M. Dunnette (Ed.) *Handbook of industrial and organisational psychology.* (pp. 1202-1245). Chicago IL: Rand McNally

Gioia, D., & Chittipeddi, K. (1991). Sensemaking and sensegiving in the strategic change initiation. *Strategic Management Journal,* 12, 433-48

Greiner, L., & Bhambri, A. (1989). New CEO intervention and dynamics of deliberate strategic change. *Strategic Management Joournal,* 10, 67-86

Graen, G & Uhl-Bien, M. (1995). Relationship-based approach to leadership: Development of leader-member exchange (LMX) theory of leadership over 25 years: Applying a multi-level, multi-domain perspective. *Leadership Quartelry,* 6(2), 219-247

Hempill, J. & Coons, A. (1957). Development of the Leader Behaviour Description Questionnaire. In R. Stogdill & A. Coons (Eds.) *Leader behaviour: Its description and measurement.* Columbus OH: Ohio State University

Hersey, P. & Blanchard, K. (1977). *Management of organisational behaviour: Utilising human resources* (3rd. ed). Engelwood Cliffs NJ: Prentice Hall

Hersey, P. & Blanchard, K. (1969). Life-cycle theory of leadership. *Training and Development Journal.* 23, 26-34

House, R. & Dressler, G. (1974). The path-goal theory of leadership: Some post hoc and a priori tests. In J. Hunt & L. Larson (Eds.) *Contingency approaches in leadership* (pp, 29-55). Carbondale IL : Southern Illinois University Press

House, R. & Mitchell, R. (1974). Path-goal theory of leadership. *Journal of Contemporary Business,* 3, 81-97

Indvik, J. (1988). *A more complete testing of path-goal theory.* Paper presented at the Academy of Management, Anaheim CA

Katz, R. (1995, January-February). Skills of an effective administrator. *Harvard Business Review*

Kets de Vries, M. (2004, January). Putting leaders on the couch. *Harvard Business Review*

Kirby, P., King, M., & Paradise, L. (1992). Extraordinary leaders in education: understanding transformational leadership. *Journal of Education Research,* 85, 303-11

Kirkpatrick, S. & Locke, E. (1991). Leadership: Do traits matter? *The Executive,* 5, 48-60

Kouzes, M. & Posner, B. (1987) *The Leadership Challenge.* San Francisco: Joey-Bass.

Kotter, J. (1990). *A force for change: How leadership differs from management.* New York NY: Free Press

Little, G. (1999). Middles way leaders. Paper delivered at the International Society of Political Psychology, Amsterdam

Lord, R., DeVarder, C., & Alliger, G. (1986). A meta-analysis of the relation between personality traits and leadership perceptions: An application of validity generalisation procedures. *Journal of Applied Psychology.* 71, 402-10

Lowe, K. & Gradner, W. (2001). Ten years of the Leadership Quarterly: Contributions and challenges for the future. *Leadership Quarterly,* 7(3), 385-9

Mant, A. (1983). *Leaders We Deserve.* Oxford: Basil Blackwell

Mant, A. (1997). *Intelligent Leadership.* St. Leonards: Allan & Unwin

Mann, R (1959). A review of the relationship between personality and performance in small groups. *Psychological Bulletin.* 56, 241-270

Mumford, M., Zaccaro, S., Harding, F., Jacobs, T. & Fleishman, E. (2000). Leadership skills for a changing world: Solving complex social problems. *Leadership Quarterly,* 11(1), 11-35

Nirenberg, J. (2001). Leadership: A practitioner's perspective on the literature. *Singapore Management Review,* 23, 1, 1-34

Northouse, P. (2004). *Leadership: Theory and Practice.* (3rd. ed.) Thousand Oaks CA: Sage Publications

Parry, K. (1998). Grounded theory and social process: a new direction for leadership research. *Leadership Quarterly* 9(1): 95-105

Pettigrew, A., & Whipp, R. (1991). *Managing change for competitive success.* Oxford: Blackwell

Reddin, W. (1967, April). The 3-D management style theory. *Training and Development Journal,* pp. 8-17

Schriesheim, C & Neider, L. (1966). Path-goal leadership theory: The long and winding road. *Leadership Quarterly,* 7(3), 317-321

Shamir, B. (1995). Social distance and charisma: theoretical notes and an exploratory study. *Leadership Quarterly* 6(1): 19-47

Sinclair, A. & Wilson, V. (2002). *New Faces of Leadership.* Melbourne: Melbourne University Press.

Steinberg, B. (1998). The making of women presidents and prime ministers: the impact of birth order, sex of siblings and parent daughter dynamics. Paper presented to the Annual Meeting of the International Society of Political Psychology, 11-15 June, Montreal

Stogdill, R. (1974). *Handbook of leadership: A survey of theory and research.* New York: Free Press

Stogdill, R. (1963). *Manual for the Leader Behaviour Description Questionnaire Form XII.* Columbus OH: Ohio State University

Stogdill, R. (1948). Personal factors associated with leadership: A survey of literature. *Journal of Psychology,* 25, 35-71

Teo, G. (2002). *Leadership and Logology.* Palmerston North: Massey University Press

Tichy, N. & DeVanna, M. (1986). *The transformational leader.* New York NY: John Wiley

Tierney, N. (1989). Symbolism and the presidential perceptions of leadership. *Review of Higher education,* 12, 153-66

Yammarino, F. (2000), Leadership skills: Introducing and overview. *Leadership Quarterly,* 11(1), 5-9

Yukl, G. (1994). *Leadership in Organizations.* New York: Prentice Hall

Zalenzik, A. (1977). Managers and Leaders: Are they different? *Harvard Business Review.* 55(2): 67-78